POETIC ENRICHMENT

Edited by

Andrew Head

First published in Great Britain in 1999 by
POETRY NOW
Remus House,
Coltsfoot Drive,
Woodston,
Peterborough, PE2 9JX
Telephone (01733) 898101
Fax (01733) 313524

All Rights Reserved

Copyright Contributors 1999

HB ISBN 0 75430 613 5
SB ISBN 0 75430 612 7

FOREWORD

Although we are a nation of poetry writers we are accused of not reading poetry and not buying poetry books: after many years of listening to the incessant gripes of poetry publishers, I can only assume that the books they publish, in general, are books that most people do not want to read.

Poetry should not be obscure, introverted, and as cryptic as a crossword puzzle: it is the poet's duty to reach out and embrace the world.

The world owes the poet nothing and we should not be expected to dig and delve into a rambling discourse searching for some inner meaning.

The reason we write poetry (and almost all of us do) is because we want to communicate: an ideal; an idea; or a specific feeling. Poetry is as essential in communication, as a letter; a radio; a telephone, and the main criteria for selecting the poems in this anthology is very simple: they communicate.

CONTENTS

Title	Author	Page
A Christmas Message	Doreen Petherick	1
This Affair	Emma-Louise Cartwright	2
In The Cellar Of My Mind	Iris Williams	3
Friends	Will Turner	4
A Tragic Recipe	A Branthwaite	5
Untitled	P Allen	6
The Stare	Joan Blisset	7
Winter Solstice	Judy Studd	8
Fallen Giant	John Norman-Daley	10
I am A Crooked Tree	Jessie Lamont	12
Bully	Deborah Butler	13
Going Away	Daniel Baker	14
Army Padre	Margaret Upson	15
The Struggle For Independence	Khan Singh Kumar	16
Universal Declaration of Human Frights	T Burke	17
Memories	Nicola Jayne Simms	18
Global Destruction	David Richards	19
Resolution	Fiona M Reid	20
A Prayer To The Christian God	Nicholas Howard	21
A Not Forgotten Past	Lydia Thomas	22
Oh Sad Little Tramp	Sylvia Radford	24
Alone	Sonia Hall	25
Purple Shadows	Kathleen Bates	26
Christmas Past, Present And Future	Dinah Pye	27
What Is Love?	Simon Warren	28
Hurting	Maureen Watson	29
Spare A Thought	N Carruthers	30
Take Me Back . . .	Joe Hughes	31
Rejection	Kate Tavener	32
Blues In The Night	Richard Stoker	33
Deanne	Brenda Dove	34
Garden Of Eden	Robert D Shooter	35
Farmer's Lament	Gillian S Roberts	36
Out Of Reach	Caroline J Sammout	37

Eleven, Eleven, Eleven Blues	Maureen Atkin	38
Lost Youth!	A Elliott	39
Blizzard Blues	Hilary Jill Robson	40
Cold Mornin' Blues	Joyce Hockley	42
Post-Op Blues	Beryl M Smith	43
The Blues	Royston E Herbert	44
A Golden Dream	Jim Sargant	45
Singing The Blues	Ivy Cawood	46
The Get Down And Blame Yourself Blues	Phoenix Martin	47
Famine!	M E White	48
Bye Bye Blues Blues . . .	Nick Spargo	49
Blues . . .	Thomas Rist	50
Poets Sing The Blues	V G Walker	51
Early Morning Blues . . .	Dennis Packham	52
Alone And Blue	Susan Mullinger	53
Lonesome Blues!	Joy Benford	54
Gone Away . . .	Alan Smith	55
Little Twin Lost	Margaret Andrews	57
My Girlfriend Is Dead!	Keith L Powell	58
Cheating Woman Blues . . .	Marcus Tyler	59
Four Times Redundant - Past It - Job Seeker Blues	Mike Jackson	60
Stroke Of Midnight Blues	Paul Wilkins	61
Sweet Melodies	Kate Susan Douglas	62
In The Rut Of The Working Class	J R Griffiths	63
Fine Lady	Marda	64
Ragtime City Blues	Alma Mongomery Frank	65
Rosa Canina	Anita Richards	66
Happier Times	Rob Herd	67
Your Love Stands Eternally	Jacqui Haynes	68
Tomorrow Comes	Kim Montia	69
Cumbria	J D Bailey	70
Gentle Whispers	Kathleen M Scatchard	71
Vapour Trails	Jack Pritchard	72
Grains Of Sand	Doreen Fraser	73
Anti-Smoking Jingles	Robert Catlin	74

That Infamous Day In 1941	Edward G Scullion	77
A Mind Full Of You . . .	Emma Clark	78
On The Eve . . .	John Dixon	79
To Our Children	Georgina Knight	80
Two Sides Of The Coin Spoilt	Joan Smith	81
And So You Become My Obsession	Kelvin Hughes	82
Shadow Of Death	Carole Saberton	84
Wandering Thoughts	A I Darwin	85
Lost Love	J J S Clare	86
The Tears I Cry . . .	Rosemary Thomson	87
In My Dreams	Margaret Banfield	88
Storm Dog	Gill Shutt	89
The Lover	David Kellard	90
A Womb With A View . . .	D Winder	92
The Last Goodbye	Margaret Luckett-Curtis	94
The Mirror	Kaja Jarosz	95
Feeling Inferior - Feeling Superior	C Sharrock	96
A Slightly Broken Man . . .	Alan Parr	97
In The Key Of Love	Anna Louise Simpson	98
Picture Negative	John Bicker	100
War And Trouble	Lachlan Taylor	101
Stukas At 8 O'Clock and 4 O'Clock	Ian R Margetts	102
On The Sweet Couch Of Youth	John Parry	104
Fall	James Conder	106
Gita . . .	Graham Hardie	108
Love Match	Richard Clewlow	110
The Things I Wish I Knew	Marion Schoeberlein	111
More Time	Carolyn Long	112
We Live In Difficult Times . . .	Antonio Martorelli	113
Confusion	Jean Paisley	114
Aberfan	Cyril George Button	115
To A Very Special Mum And Dad	Julie Wilkins	116
Cats And Dogs	Michelle Widdrington	118
Children!	David Strauss Steer	119

Insiders	Kenneth Wilcox	120
Rhapsody Of The Rat Race	Sean Conway	121
To A Young German Sailor	John Finch	122
Mother's Room . . .	Derek (Dovann) Blackburn	123
This Easter	Kendric Ross	124

A Christmas Message

Three shepherds sat around their fire,
High upon a hill,
Ice cold was the night,
Their flocks lay very still.
A pale blue sky and a mellow moon,
The stars were shining bright,
When suddenly, the shepherds saw
A vivid, brilliant light.
And an angel did appear,
'Fear not,' said he,
'Be not afraid
To you I bring good cheer.
Arise, I say and travel far,
Guided by the Eastern Star.
For in a stable, swathed in swaddling clothes
A babe is born in Bethlehem, Judea.
This message unto you I bring
Jesus Christ, our Saviour King is here.'

Doreen Petherick

THIS AFFAIR

It cannot go on,
This affair that we have looked upon
As passing like the flash bulb's glare
Caught swinging in the tightrope
Air where you, wrapped
Your legs around me, spring's lamb
Suckling at my neck, the vein rising to
Your lips, a straw into my strawberry
Milkshake heart that sips
My 'kiss me' breast woke up for this.

You were the meeting on the stairs,
Footprints first onto the sand,
Washed out in the saliva sea,
Warm oyster mouths
You swallowed me with acid tang
You tasted deep
Unshelled love, soft, we chewed away
Crustacae years, clasp opened
Pearls untouched as tears,
But it cannot go on,
This life we lead.

Emma-Louise Cartwright

IN THE CELLAR OF MY MIND

Whom do I talk to
When I think I am insane
The only intelligent person
Is myself of course, inane
Conversation to me will be unknown

Why am I unhappy
Self actualisation wanting higher goals
Disorientated neurotic psychotic
Is this thought transference
Misinterpretation schizophrenic
Because I'm too damned old

Suddenly a wondrous stated of Euphoria
Intelligence has succumbed
No more suffering from paranoia
Or deterioration within the brain
Insanity is now inanity
In the cellar of my mind.

Iris Williams

FRIENDS

Think back to the good times,
the inspirations then, captured
with the love of life, no doubt
to comprehend.
Bring those good times forward
to help to continue anew,
to get you through the harsher days
undoubtedly not so blue.

I hate to see complacency, it did
not come from me, you've been
the best of them all, a pal
who set me free.
I'm different from the others, I am
only but true, there's nothing in
the world I'd do, to ever upset you.

I think of only lasting friendship,
never to let go, I never knew
anyone like you, please never ever go.
I'm not an instigator, can't profess
to certain things, that's why I've
had to state my case; because of
what your friendship means.

Will Turner

A Tragic Recipe

Take one neglected child, ignore it.
Allow it to simmer with a touch of bitterness.
Reject all available talent, allow to cool for several years.
Mix freely with criminal fraternities until proficient.

Beat the contents well until full of despair.
Fragment and crush the despondent soul.
Bake in an oven of apathy and hatred.
Repeat the recipe until society learns a lesson.

A Branthwaite

UNTITLED

The act of a mad man
made him a sad man
All that learning
wasted in time
Unemployment
turned him to rhyme
Many years have come
and gone
See that sad man
turn to Rome
He still dreams
of going back
and it's this alone
that keeps him on track

P Allen

THE STARE

He was there, every day
He was there staring
Bleary-eyed blank and white.
I saw his plight, Should I help?
I thought I should, yet wasn't sure.
Yes, I'd help. I knew I would.
He knew it too. He'd notice me
Looking his way each day.
December was bleak, the trees were bare.
My God his stare! Blank! Blank! Blank!
It got to me. I felt a cause coming on.
Patronisingly I stared at him
In his place on the pavement.
He looked a fixture.
'Did he ever move?' I wondered.
He realised my thoughts.
He winked - a cheeky wink.
Not so blank. A soul inside a dirty sack.
He'd stared me back!
Speech? Was that there? Should I care?
I did. I know I did.

Joan Blisset

Winter Solstice

Through England's bleak mid-winter
The cold, the frost and snow
The void was filled with fairy lights
The darkness was aglow
They wallowed in wild parties
They swallowed up large beer
Bedecked the trees with tinsel
And Santas drove reindeer
For Jesus was a legend
And Father Christmas real
They all conceived a fable
With a backdrop surreal
Stonehenge still stood; the answer?
For tangible it seems
But stones alone yield coldness
An idol Druid's dream.

In England's bleak mid-winter
The people groaned and moaned
Were searching for reality
Yet searching for a stone
The truth is set before them
The way is clear and bright
So . . . why are they still groping
And searching for that light
The truth has always been there
'Midst mistletoe and holly
And Jesus gives eternal life
Not Santa Claus so jolly.

The key has been provided
No mere ephemeral stone
Or other transient objects
To worship as a throne
The door to Heaven's open
Symbolic as the star
Which led wise men to Jesus
And shepherds from afar
At last there was an answer
To Man's incessant sin
The door is standing open
And peace is found within
The saddest song is Solstice
The pagan's heartfelt cry
Rejection of the way and truth
But they were sold a lie.

Judy Studd

FALLEN GIANT

Once a giant who many feared,
now he old and grey in beard,
and for him no respect have the young,
as he wanders through them.
But many a tale can he tell,
of waiting for the opening bell,
getting up - 'seconds out,'
for another fighting bout.
He would take them all on,
               young and old,
when he raised those fists,
               the blood went cold,
completely fearless, and non-sympathetic,
the giant he so athletic.
Inside those ropes he was at home,
not safe for other men to roam,
he would go through them like a
               knife through butter,
and was he the greatest upper-cutter?
They came from all over, land and sea,
to see him bring opponents to their knees,
his excellent composure and perfect stance,
no other fighter had a chance.
A gruesome sight to those who
               feared blood,
he would spoil the features
             that once looked good.

Though despite those many great battles he won,
now his riches have all gone,
his shoulders are sunken, his legs are bent,
he's just another tired old gent.
For it's over thirty years since he
                        hung up his gloves,
and said goodbye to the sport he loves,
yet though he never fought again,
he remains a legend to many men.

John Norman-Daley

I Am A Crooked Tree

I am a crooked tree
That once was tall and strong.
I can no longer see,
Nor hear a simple song.

I live within my mind
With it I wander far
Where the wild streams wind
And where the hawthorns are.

The sea at its full tide
Will wait for me a while,
And nothing bright will hide
That used to make me smile.

Jessie Lamont

BULLY
(Written on my 9th birthday)

Why are you picking on me, what did I do,
I only want to be your friend and to play with you.
It's not very nice standing in this schoolyard all on my own,
Except for your taunts of laughter I feel ever so alone.

I know I look a little different, not how you think I should be,
But I really am a beautiful person, if only you could see.
Each day in the dinner line, I'm always at the end,
When all I ever really want is for you to be my friend.

I'm not a monster, just someone to call, someone to laugh at,
I just want to be a part of your games and all of that,
Please don't pull my hair again, please give me back my book,
Please don't throw that stone, it's not my fault for the way that I look.

Please think before you decide what to say,
Please, not just now, you see it's my birthday,
Please don't kick and push at me, please don't make me cry,
Now I feel as I did yesterday - like I want to die.

Try to understand that your childhood doesn't become
                                                      a thing of the past,
The memories stay with you and forever they last,
So wouldn't you rather play with me today and share a happy time,
So that when I'm all grown up I can look at you and say
      'There goes a friend of mine.'

Deborah Butler

GOING AWAY

When you're not around
The birds don't sing
The sun doesn't shine
The phones don't ring
My head's not mine
When you're not around

When you're not around
The breeze turns cold
The river won't flow
The stories are all told
But you'll never know
When I'm not around

When I'm not around
The children'll still play
The birds'll sing a sweeter song
The clouds'll go away
'Cause you'll still go on
When I'm not around

Daniel Baker

ARMY PADRE

He laid down in a dirty trench
Among wounded men English and French
He hated the dreadful war
All the terrible killings he saw
He thought of things through his pain
In the trench he would remain
A lot of men were already dead
To be taken prisoner others dread
Bombs dropped on left to right
Guns thundered day and night
Then someone else in the trench fell
Causing him to move and yell
He prayed to God to help the poor soul
Who had fallen into the dark hole
From his pocket he took his cross and book
Around the trench he started to look
He knew in his leg he had been shot
And a lot of pain he got
But it was the work for God he must do
And pray for the others and God's help to see them through
Lame, thinner, they were home at last
He thanked God the war was gone so fast
For the people with him in the war
He welcomed them through his church door.

Margaret Upson

THE STRUGGLE FOR INDEPENDENCE

I knew my friends after Gandhi's death,
in the Economics A' Level lesson,
in the heated sidetrack, my Sikh mate
Kaz - offended by my need to study
('Think you're white, don't you? Well Jut-boy,
there's a shadow hanging over us - even you!')
tore into his own rhetoric.
He just couldn't see why the front door to our house
was more literal than his could often be,
where it opened was where it shut,
and when that summer
when the Hindu boys and the Sikh boys,
in their car parks and on their Broadways
played out a blood-bath
until both claimed victory,
and when the night out at Slough Cannon,
when Kaz and his dapple shadowed gang
where the neon missed them,
saw me heading for their long queue
then turn from it, coming after me
they surged the wind in a blow-back:
Oi, coconut!
      Coconut!
           Coconut!
                kicking into my stride
I couldn't tell if they were too
to the dark of the car park
where the claims for Ayodhya
would hinge once again on fealty

(realising I'd left Tom behind)

Khan Singh Kumar

UNIVERSAL DECLARATION OF HUMAN FRIGHTS

'Born equal', but some appear with silver spoons in their mouths!
Many, defunct of feeling, wallow in consciences of liquid mercury.
'Let religion, colour, birth or status prop the system!' spells doubts,
To let opponents rot in prison is the current price of uneasy victory.

Anyone who mocks the state has no right to enjoy life or freedom.
Keep doubters enslaved to serve the nation till they just fade or die.
Whip and torture those who show audacity to anchor public reason.
Manipulate the law with impunity so cool courage must swiftly fly.

Produce patrols of perdition to patrol the paths with pistols drawn.
Those who disagree are guilty with future fortunes locked in bond.
Confiscate property and wealth so that they feel the crown of thorn.
Cage closest relatives to ensure their children are loath to abscond!

Jobs for loyal retainers so let dissidents languish in barbed camps.
Apostles are worthy of inflated wages so stamp heretics underrate.
Those too weak to oppose must drift like nomads, asylum tramps.
Ration essential food supplies to let their progeny eat a cruel fate.

Education is a special privilege so deny it to all obdurate objectors.
Forbid opponents to marry for their future offspring are anathema.
Only lovers of the party shall wear the exalted halo of protectors.
'Holy adulation' is the only way that ambitious backs gain stamina!

T Burke

MEMORIES

I need some time
I need some space
To get away from my heart and mind
I can't take it any more I'm going insane
Thinking of you if you're thinking of me
Spending together for eternity

There's one thing special, so deep in my heart
It's you I'm thinking of my one true love
Your eyes are so clear; there's nothing to hide
I think of your smile that lightens my life
I know you're from heaven near hell bound
Your voice is like an angel that's sent from the skies
Or were you a vision from my own eyes

Nicola Jayne Simms

GLOBAL DESTRUCTION

The rainforests once covered the Earth
just grew and grew for all its worth,
all kinds of creatures lived there in peace
utilising bushes, trees, filling every niche,
a variety of species, animals and plants
rare flowers, orang-utan, to millions of ants,
to name but a few, this was home to them all
then along came man, and man had a ball,
chopped at the trees, threw rubbish everywhere
released harmful gases into the air,
hunted and killed, destroyed all he could find
just laughing it off, with never no mind,
millions of hectares are burnt every year
leaving creatures and man, living in fear,
burning fossil fuels, does not help at all
but talking to man, is like talking to the wall,
with the rain falling on barren land
causing mud slides that bury homes, animals and man,
killing all plants for farm cattle to graze
fills me with anger, fills me with rage,
all this destruction to satisfy man's needs
will be the death of this Earth, for the sake of greed.

David Richards

RESOLUTION

I am going to be free
Of his all-consuming control
I am going to be *me,*
Never more shall I be in his thrall.

Leave me alone with my life
To recover myself and be whole,
I am no longer your wife!
To be treated as one with no soul.

I am going to be loved
With no precondition attached
No price will have to be paid
For the giving away of my heart.

I am going to be wooed
By someone to whom I'll come first
I'll be fêted and dined and pursued,
Only my love will assuage his thirst.

Yes! I am going to be free
I'll be cherished, admired and enjoyed.
Now I shall truly be *me*
My spirit has not been destroyed.

Fiona M Reid

A Prayer To The Christian God

Dear Lord I confess I am confused
I have read your testaments and creeds
And I have listened to your disciples
It seems that you and your father are one
So his mistress your mother must be your mistress too
You created the world
But deny responsibility for its faults
You rectified the design by father-self killing son-self
This same son who was born of an adulterous liaison
With the consent of the cuckolded fiance
Infanticide spices up this plot
When necromancy stirs the dead to life
We are told God is love
And in your merciful name your followers
Torture maim and kill inconvenient critic voices
Horde wealth, hate niggers, whores and queers
For two millennia then revise selected eternal verities
And disavow the troublesome past
But still bless wars and succour killers, liars, and cheats
By eating flesh and drinking blood you celebrate yourself
And in your church embrace all that which hurts and harms
But spew the intensity of your venom to this day
At the love of man for man or woman for woman
The tenderness and joy of a same sex rapport
Is abhorrent in your eyes and you reserve
The savagest condemnation for life enhancing love
Dear Lord I confess I am confused.

Nicholas Howard

A NOT FORGOTTEN PAST

Not a home with great conveniences
Had I when newly wed,
A cold lino floor greeted a toe
When rising from one's bed.

First task of day, get fire in play
In the large black-leaded grate,
For kettle to boil and bacon to fry
With the eggs for breakfast plate.

On hooks in the kitchen ceiling
Was bacon and ham on display,
Pre-salted in brine in the dairy
That stood in for fridge in that day.

Soda, the agent for grease one used
When doing the washing up chore,
Then on one's knees one had to scrub
The flagstone kitchen floor.

Electricity still had not arrived
In that farmhouse home for me,
So a daunting task was washing day
With roughness of hands the fee.

A coal-fired boiler in outhouse
Was centre of Monday's scene,
Along with the old scrubbing board
To get dirty linen clean.

No step into shower or even a bath
After chores on such heavy a day,
Hot water to take to basin upstairs
And wash down in primitive way.

For Saturday night was bathing night,
To be clean for the Sabbath day,
Kettles of water to fill the tin tub
Then a soak by the fire, the way.

Behind the house, up the garden
Was 'Ty Bach' as known in Wales,
A bench with two holes - double toilet
And beneath - two 'empty job' pails.

Lucky for me, five years on set free
From that hand erosion life
New house with power and some mod cons
Brought bliss to a thankful wife.

In case I forgot, there's reminder 'neath pot
Of the bakestone I used long ago,
Flat irons as well, evoke an old smell
With a scorching, burst forth of *oh no!*

Memories there, when I stand and stare
And note all the comforts around,
To appreciate that the black-leaded grate
Gave me feet that were firm on the ground.

Lydia Thomas

OH SAD LITTLE TRAMP

Sitting on his park bench
Watching the world go by
The gaunt little figure
With the staring, doleful eyes.
I wonder what he's thinking
As he stares out into space
When dreamy lovers pass him
At their casual, leisurely pace.
Or he sees the little children
Raucously delighted
Running around in play
Loved, protected and excited.
But security is not his
With his belongings in a bag
He sits on his park bench
Smoking a dog-end for a fag.
Oh sad little tramp
Would your life you rise above
If help were offered to you
Would you accept a home and love.

Sylvia Radford

ALONE

Will we meet again?
Will our tranquil minds . . .
Rendezvous across
the sands of time . . . ?

Will our thoughts renew
sweet memories of joy . . .
entering worlds . . .
yet unseen, except
in our secret dreams?

Will our loving hearts
cry out and open
arms, yearn to fill
the empty sterile spaces?

Will it always be
a vigil of One . . . ?
Mourning the loss
of 'we'
Once, 'all one'

Now . . . just me . . .
'Alone'
a part of nothing?

Sonia Hall

PURPLE SHADOWS

How can I write of
Old age, that day
Seen far off, stealthily
    It came
A purple shadow
Across the open page.
How bright the stars
With shadows in flight
Through the vast hills
Where the wind rides west
Through the rust and gold
    Of autumn leaves
The eternal silent pattern
    Nature weaves
The twinkle in the eye
Dies in a weariness
For the heart grieves
    Till winter's frost
In glittering mask
    Walks quietly
Through the rust and gold
Old Father Time calling
Autumn leaves, one by one
    Gently falling
Where purple shadows passed.

Kathleen Bates

CHRISTMAS PAST, PRESENT AND FUTURE
(A dedication to my family and friends - Christmas 1998)

Christmas Past: Christmas is here
Another year
Gone forever!
Shed a tense tear
For loved ones dear
Gone forever!
I hear you sigh
Good times past by
Gone forever!

Christmas Present: On Christmas morn
Jesus was born
Here forever!
Time to believe
Love to receive
Here forever!
Sins to be shed
Good times ahead
Here forever!

Christmas Future: New Year begins
A fresh start brings
Hope forever!
What pains we feel
Together - we'll
Hope forever!
Through life's cruel sea
There has to be
Hope forever!

Dinah Pye

WHAT IS LOVE?

People going at it hammer and tongs
The kind of tension which is electric
And the space everybody needs
I ran away from school
I ran away from work
I run away from people
Yet outside it all
One has a regard for human nature
The distance is all
Perhaps a little song will do
Those I think of are too old to dance
Though lost in the mists of time
They danced
They loved and were loved in turn
Whilst others
Lived out their lives alone
Too timid ever to get involved
The spinsters and bachelors of this parish
Time and space, whirl around these homes
The singular nature of the men
I want to make a dedication
To the people in my life
I've been wary of them all
Which is how I place them
Like marionettes dancing jerkily
To a tune the rhythm of which
Always out-speeded their ability
As though their strings were being jerked too hard
The parting is meaningless
Disappearance all

Simon Warren

HURTING

Where are you my friend, you've been gone quite a while,
Where have you travelled to, you've been gone a fair while,
Oh how I miss your spontaneous smile.

We met every day, we discussed everything,
Every day we united to discuss everything
And sometimes we talked and sometimes we'd sing.

Two minds as one our thoughts converged,
Two souls together, our ideas converged,
Beyond expectations, our friendship surged.

Life was a happiness, blessed and unfailing,
Life was contentment, favoured, unfailing.
The future decreed all set for plain sailing.

A lone disagreement, unswerving, unkind,
A lone altercation unwavering, unkind.
Headstrong, inflexible, no change of mind.

No conversation, the days were too long,
No rendezvous, the weeks were too long,
I've had time to realise that I've been so wrong.

I cannot remember the harsh words we said,
I cannot recall the cruel things I said,
And so you departed and filled me with dread.

Where are you my friend, you've been gone quite a while,
Where have you travelled to, you've been a fair while,
Oh, how I miss your spontaneous smile.

Maureen Watson

SPARE A THOUGHT

Christmas cards lots of holly
Deck the halls let's be jolly
Put the tree up light it well
Party time we'll look swell
But don't forget those without
Don't give to get
That's what Christmas is about
Homeless people children too
Spare them a thought
That's not hard to do
They need our help
In more ways than one
Give them some time
You can still have your fun.

N Carruthers

TAKE ME BACK . . .

Take me back to the womb I was wise then.
Take me back to my childhood
And lies then.

Take me back to my school time and blues time.
Take me back to my college
And curse them.

Take me back to my mother most Catholic.
Take me back to the priests
Most fanatic.

Take me back to my job and my prison.
Take me back to the church -
No religion.

Take me back to old age I'm despised now.
Take me back to the grave -
No more poise now!

Joe Hughes

Rejection

Mauve to nightmare purple
Oilskin sleek
I slip through tulip curves
Speed outstrips
Control
Earth's pull
Upon my helpless heels
Exerts a force of unleashed fury
Your eyes, matt grey
Unfocussed slate
Slivers from The Principality
Belie your words which spew
The hopeless froth of scorn
Upon my ears
Deceit masquerades
Behind a face of faux sincerity
Apologies
Fall freely
Off disdainful lips
Each syllable a poisoned dart
Down I slide
Discarded,
Compost through the shoot
Lungs compressed
By damning pain engorged with lead
The indescribable
Crushes my breast to pulp
And blood seeps silently
Through pores
To mingle with my tears.

Kate Tavener

BLUES IN THE NIGHT

I'll never be young again
I'll never see eighteen
Or all that time in between.

It'll never rain on me
It'll never snow
This makes me feel so low.

The thought that I'll not run
The thought that I'll not swim
Drives me to the rim.

I'll never see life again
I'll never feel love
Or fly through those clouds above.

My mind is free once more
My fancies free to dream
I'll never more be mean

I'll write it here for you to read
I'll write it out for you to sing
And in that way I'll hear life's changes ring.

Richard Stoker

DEANNE

I'd like to give a friend a present
Because of her kind temperament
A gift of what?
It's troubling me
I'll use my pen for discovery
Words say more than glitzy wrappings
Words aren't cheap or temptingly fattening
Leave no stains or lingering hangovers
Or accost the nose with obdurate odours
They don't need to be size 12 or 14
Nor any trace of a high from caffeine

So coffee and clothes and scents for your nose
Chocolates and wine and truffles sublime
You'll need to discover under the tree
'Cos you ain't getting them from me!
Just a giggle from a friendly crank
A simple page with a word of thanks
And future friendship - you and me.

Brenda Dove

GARDEN OF EDEN
(Dedicated to Kent Nagano)

Messien's Saint Francis, establishing
proper quality of the silences,
Kent - personal story demonstrating
composer's insistence on nuances
being environmentally the right
timbre for that quiet. You see that one
reveals the ascending Jesus, his light
must thus shine through this space, special, felt zone.
Yet now it is his spirit, or body
coming fresh off the Cross, all done for us,
essential each silence echoes what He
did for us, goes with Christ, lived by use. Thus
we too in Halle Choir - orchestra - all -
must share that eternal journey - our call.

Robert D Shooter

FARMER'S LAMENT

A farmer's life can be tough,
A farmer's life is often tough
But farming's their love, however rough.

Farmers often drive big cars,
Farmers often drive dirty big cars,
Even drive cars with roo bars!

Farming was a happy way of life,
No longer is it a happy way of life,
It is heartbreaking form-filling strife.

Farmers often cry wolf they say,
Farmers always cry wolf they say,
Now it's time for them to pay!

What do we care the public cries,
We don't care, we won't hear their cries,
We don't care if farming dies.

We'll import food at a cost,
The more we import, the more the cost,
We don't care if farming's lost.

Farmers will have to try to survive,
Farmers will fight to try to survive,
Fight to keep the countryside alive.

Gillian S Roberts

OUT OF REACH

Do you ever get that feeling stirring deep within?
It makes way unashamedly and fills our heads with sin.
Heartbeats sound like bass drums, pounding through my mind.
Inhaling deepest potent breaths, these thoughts I must defy.
Not one to be so forward, behind the smile I hide,
You'll never know the war I face against the urge inside.
Rapid breathing rages, confusing every word.
I want to grasp and take you now but that would be absurd.
Instead I look you in the eye and watch your every move,
Satisfied with what I see, you've nothing more to prove.
But who am I to think this way, to have this fantasy?
I'll never be as special . . . what would he see in me?

Caroline J Sammout

ELEVEN, ELEVEN, ELEVEN BLUES

Woke up this morning, from dreams of years long gone,
this dismal morning, from dreams of times long gone.
Those days are distant, but memories linger on.

I lay, reflecting, on those traumatic years,
so quiet, reflecting, on past traumatic years.
Soon my reflections gave way to floods of tears.

My recollections echoed with bombs of war,
when air-raid sirens warned of those bombs of war,
this child not knowing what folk were fighting for.

Too many people, some they were oh, so young,
many fine people gave up their lives so young
to halt cruel Hitler who aimed to do us wrong.

They're not forgotten, all those who fought and died,
no, not forgotten, those who were maimed and died.
Their friends and families, my how they mourned and cried.

I'm weeping too, now, this bleak November day,
weeping salt tears, now, this sad November day,
for those proud warriors whose lives were blown away.

Each year, in silence, we pause, remembering;
one minute's silence, for quiet remembering,
seems insufficient for those who peace did bring.

They fought for glory but suffered grief and pain,
brave souls, now sleeping, they suffered so much pain.
Victorious victims, no hero died in vain.

A silent 'Thank you' is all that I can give,
a heartfelt 'Thank you' we, ever more, must give,
for sacrificing their lives that we might live.

Maureen Atkin

LOST YOUTH!

Youth on her face, like a mirror once shone,
Youth on her face that shone
It's many years since it has gone!

Years have gone and left their mark,
Years have gone, left a mark
Of deep lines like on a tree's bark!

Lines carved deep by passing time
Lines carved deep with time
By tears alone, each line!

Her beauty now tarnished alone,
Her beauty tarnished alone
Only love remains strong, not gone!

Her black eyes glint when she smiles,
Her black eyes glint, she smiles
Remembering youth, then cries!

Her tear-washed face, now dry,
Her tear-soaked face, dry
Today she's smiling, but why?

The deep scars of time past alone
The deep scars of past, alone
Will not dimmer love, that's gone.

In life's autumn she is reminiscing,
In life's autumn years, reminiscing
About her youth and beauty, now missing!

A secret burning candle in her heart,
A burning candle in the heart
Keeps her memories, never to part.

A Elliott

BLIZZARD BLUES

Blizzard blues, we were happy as romping lambs; without money
We were happy and to us all was sunny,
Day after day, sweet as honey.

Dining out with friends a rare treat,
Partying with family a rare feat,
Times together always upbeat.

Blizzard blues; scoured the decks to pay urgent fuel refills,
Searched our pockets to pay grocery bills,
To halt business sliding into foothills.

Gradually trade began to climb
Gradually wintry trade became springtime,
Victorious clock chimed in time.

Blizzard blues, overnight you showed a sudden interest in dress,
Overnight your hair styled; interest to impress,
Your feet hovered then left ground with success.

Later and later staggered home syndrome
Later and later arrival to work syndrome
Nightly with various women did roam.

Blizzard blues, with mates you headed to bars in town at sundown,
Without mates you headed to bars downtown to drown,
Your wayward ways caused us final showdown.

Pledged a promise to me to keep from brew,
Pledged promise for chance to renew
Our life, maybe love, united anew.

Blizzard blues, to regain health and self now in clinic rehab;
To regain health and self with both hands must grab
Opportunity, before we conflab.

Blizzard blues will change to summer
If you convince; no longer a bummer,
We can restore our midsummer.

Hilary Jill Robson

COLD MORNIN' BLUES

Woke up this mornin' with feelin' of dread,
just woke this mornin' with feelin' of dread -
wantin' to just stay in my bed.

Look'd out of window, saw the sky,
just look'd out, and saw that ol' sky -
somethin' in me seem'd to die.

Stumbled about, got into my clothes,
just stumbled about, and into my clothes -
didn't want to get up, goodness knows!

Put my nose out of doors, and it jus' froze,
just put my nose out, and it just froze -
my fingers were cold, and so were my toes:

How I wished I could stay in bed,
just curl up, and stay in bed,
wouldn't then have this feelin' of dread.

Joyce Hockley

POST-OP BLUES

Testing, testing, can I hold a pen?
Testing, testing, count from one to ten?
And if I can't quite manage it - what then?

Testing, testing, do I know my name?
Testing, testing, ask me that again,
Because those two short words don't sound the same.

Testing, testing, the hours that used to fly
Testing, testing, now lag and drag and sigh -
Their usefulness has gone, and pride must die.

Testing, testing, these hands that once could grasp -
Testing, testing, alas for the sweet past -
I must, reluctant, seek another's clasp.

Testing, testing - I've failed to make the grade,
Testing, testing - enough of life's parade -
It's time to be dispensed with, I'm afraid.

Beryl M Smith

THE BLUES

I've got the blues 'cos my lady's gone away
Yes I've got the blues 'cos my lady's gone away
My lady's gone away so I'm crying all the day

I lost my lady 'cos she's gone off with my friend
Oh, yes I've lost my lady 'cos she's gone off with my friend
She's gone off with my friend so my days are at an end

My lady was my lady till a month or so ago
My lady was my lady only just a while ago
Now she's gone and my days are full of woe!

I've got the blues since my lady went away
Oh, yes I've got the blues since my lady went away
She left me now I'm crying every night and every day!

My blues are still with me since my lady went away
Oh, yes my blues are still with me since my lady went away
All my life I'll be hoping that she'll be back again one day!

Royston E Herbert

A Golden Dream

I had a dream,
Had a golden dream,
I went to a place where I'd never been.

I climbed a hill,
Climbed a golden hill,
Till I reached the top, then I took my fill.

Of a wondrous sight,
Such a wondrous sight,
Saw a golden valley full of golden light.

You were waiting there,
Beauty, waiting there,
In the golden light shone your golden hair.

You said, 'Take my hand,
Come and take my hand'
Then you led me down through that golden land.

All the angels sang,
How the angels sang,
Golden eagles soared, golden church bells rang.

You were so at peace,
You were calm, at peace,
How I envied you in that golden fleece.

Wrapped so safe around,
Wrapped in love around,
Not a single fear, nor a tearful sound.

Then you said goodbye,
Then we said goodbye,
As the morning rays lit the golden skies.

Jim Sargant

SINGING THE BLUES

Oh! I'm tired of singing the blues
Can't sing, but I'm tired of singing the blues
Bills coming in - in loads - not in twos!

Naught goes right, new shoes are tight
Yes, they're tight - 'cos naught goes right
And I'll get corns - a horrid sight . . .

Blues are all wrong, but singing's alright
I'm sure blues are wrong and singing's alright
But my singing seems to make people take flight . . .

Lots of folk are singing the blues
There must be lots all singing the blues
So shriek out loud, you've nothing to lose!

Car won't go, it needs new battery
Yes! Car won't go, must get a new battery
An' mustn't forget - take cat to cattery . . .

I'm singing the blues now holiday's near
I'll sing the blues with holidays here
An' drown my sorrows in lots of beer.

Think singing the blues must be a fine art
Oh! singing the blues is sure a fine art
An' it can spoil the direction of Cupid's dart!

So make yourself heard and sing out the blues
Yes! Shout out loud those old miserable blues
'Cos nobody hears soft dove-like coos . . .

Ivy Cawood

THE GET DOWN AND BLAME YOURSELF BLUES

The wind outside is howling, howling like my heart;
a wind outside is howling - it can't match my heart . . .
because that poor soul's been howling since our love fell apart.

Garbage blowing round the street, clutt'ring up my mind;
garbage blowing round the street, there's no sense to find.
Trash is messin' up my head because you were so unkind.

Coldness in the air, like the words which killed my soul;
coldness in the air, my sweet - like a big black hole!
When it comes to cruel baby - you have the starring role!

How did you get so callous, did you hate me so?
Was I just useless ballast - did you hate me so?
Did your friends revile me, or were you glad to see me go?

There's screaming in my head, babe - screams through night and day;
a screaming in my head which just won't go away!
Couldn't you, wouldn't you . . . why didn't I force you to stay!
Well! Couldn't you, wouldn't you . . . why didn't I force you to stay!

Phoenix Martin

FAMINE!

I was queuing up for my bread one day
Then I queued up again to keep hunger at bay
'Twas famine time, what more can I say?

So hot and dry, no sign of rain,
I keep on queuing again and again.
I wonder, will my queuing be in vain?

M E White

BYE BYE BLUES BLUES . . .

I bought a lott'ry ticket an' you know the damn' thing won!
I said I bought a lott'ry ticket an' you know the damn' thing won.
Now everybody tells me I'm a lucky son of a gun!

I got a lot o' money, but I still can't shake these blues,
You know I got a lot o' money, but I still can't shake these blues,
'Cos everybody an' his brother wants me to pay their dues.

Before I had this money life was really such a gas,
Before I had this money, life was such a crazy gas,
Now everyone's a grifter and they're all after my ass.

I thought I'd be so happy, but I'm really feelin' down,
Thought I'd be so happy, but I'm feelin' twelve feet down,
Gonna pack a lightweight suitcase, catch a plane an' blow this town.

I guess you think I'm foolish an' I'm doin' somethin' rash
I bet you say I'm bein' foolish an' I'm doin' somethin' rash,
But don't you worry 'bout me, 'cos I've still got all that cash.

I bought a lott'ry ticket an' you know the damn' thing won,
I said I bought a lott'ry ticket an' you know the damn' thing won,
Now I'm here in Monte Carlo - an' I'm really havin' fun . . .

Nick Spargo

BLUES...

I'm thinking about you,
I'm thinking about you
In pornographic blue.

Your thoughts almost see-through,
Your thoughts almost see through,
Your stupid hat askew.

You smile, and then it's true,
You smile, and then it's true?
The wind tugging at you.

I guess I always knew,
I guess I always do,
Beside the blue sea, blue.

Thomas Rist

POETS SING THE BLUES

Why aren't you here - I need you?
Why aren't you here - and true?
Without your life is oh so hard - and ever blue.

Why did you leave - without a care?
Why did you leave me - to despair?
Without you life is oh so hard - and so unfair.

Don't you know still - that I love you?
Don't you know - no matter what you do?
Without your life is oh so hard - and ever blue . . .

V G Walker

EARLY MORNING BLUES . . .

Woke up this morning and I was all alone
Yeah! woke up this morning and I was all alone
My bed was empty for my woman she had gone . . .

My mind was worried, oh what had I done
Said my mind was worried, oh what had I done!
I'd only been out drinking, had me a little fun . . .

I got to thinking - just what can I do?
Well! I got to thinking - just what can I do!
Guess I'll find another woman and get over you . . .

So I ain't gonna let it, let it worry me
Said I ain't gonna let it, let it worry me!
The folks all tell me there's more fish in the sea . . .

Things ain't easy, just ain't been going my way
No! Things ain't easy, just ain't been going my way!
But the sun's gonna shine in my back door someday . . .

I'm gonna get up and put on my blue suede shoes
So I'm gonna get up and put on my blue suede shoes!
Gonna go downtown and lose these early morning blues . . .

Dennis Packham

ALONE AND BLUE

I've been left alone feeling blue,
I've been left alone without you
And now whatever will I do?

You have gone and left me alone,
You have gone, left me on my own.
You packed your bags and left my home.

How will I cope without you here?
How will I cope without you near?
Please tell me I've nothing to fear.

What did I do that was so wrong?
What did I do because you've gone!
I want you back I sing in song.

I've been left alone feeling blue,
I've been left alone without you,
And now whatever will I do?

Susan Mullinger

Lonesome Blues!

I used to feel fine
I felt real fine
When my baby was mine
I drank too much wine
Too much wine
I was way out of line
I couldn't see
No I couldn't see
What it was doing to me
I thought I was strong
I was so strong
But God! I was wrong
I heard the bell
The loud door bell
I felt like hell
She was outside
She stood outside
I had no more pride
I asked for a date
Just one more date
She said 'You're too late!'

Joy Benford

GONE AWAY . . .

Now you've gone and left me
Now you've gone away
Wherever you've gone and wherever you are -
my love for you will stay.

Alan Smith

LITTLE TWIN LOST

Little twin my dog has left me - she is gone, my toy - my five pounds
bundle of joy.
Little twin my Yorkie has left me - not here - she is gone, my toy, my
five pounds bundle of joy.
We were like two peas in a pod, now not two but one.
Please announce this on that giant tannoy . . .

Did you see where she went to? Steel blue and tan?
Did you see where she skipped off to? Small, steel blue and tan?
Was she taken by a small boy, a girl, youth, woman or man?

Somebody must have taken a liking to her - that's all I can say
Somebody without a heart must have taken a liking to her - cruel -
that's all I can say.
If this person has a heart, please return her, I'm poor - but shall pay . . .

She used to be so frisky, pert and happy-go-lucky
She used to be alert, sad - she's now gone - so happy-go-lucky
I'm so unlucky - she's gone far - far away from her pleasant home
in Kentucky!

I looked at the *lost and found* columns of the newspapers today
I perused at the *lost and found* columns of the newspapers today
No mention of Twinnie, my little dog, my pet, not here but a lonely,
forgotten stray . .

Perhaps some kind soul has found her and she is his now for keeps
Perhaps a kind person has found her and now *owns* her - is his now
for keeps!
I sit here and cry - he would return her to me if he only knew how
her owner weeps . . .

Worse still, has she been put down - dead and fast asleep?
Worse still, has Twinnie been killed, dead and fast asleep!
Won't somebody tell me, enlighten me? As my pain is so very deep . . .

I look up at the stars - it's been two years now
I look up at the stars, not a twinkle, no Twinnie - it's been two
                                                                            years now
And wonder - has somebody killed her? Why, where and how?

I wipe my eyes, blood red and I cannot sleep
I dry my eyes, blood red, awake and I still cannot sleep
Is Twinnie forever sleeping - nobody can console me
I shall forever weep . . .

Margaret Andrews

My Girlfriend Is Dead!

My girlfriend is dead
But my girlfriend should have lived instead
So we could get wed
Tomorrow some time . . .

My girlfriend is dead
Did my girlfriend have such a big head?
Some say that it was filled with lead
Ready for marrying me some time tomorrow . . .

My girlfriend is dead
So a new girlfriend I must find to take to bed
Then after see if me she will wed
Some time after tomorrow . . .

Keith L Powell

CHEATING WOMAN BLUES . . .

My baby, you gone left me, packed your bags, walked out the door,
My baby, you gone left me, packed your bags, walked out the door,
You walked out on me baby, 'cos you don't need me no more.

You walked out this morning, left me in misery and pain,
You walked out this morning, left me in misery and pain.
Even though you a two-timing woman, I want you back again.

You left me standing in the cold, another man you gonna wed,
You left me standing in the cold, another man you gonna wed.
Even though you shattered my heart, I can't get you out my head.

What we had was such a sweet thing, now you gone done me wrong,
What we had was such a sweet thing, now you gone done me wrong.
You walked out on me darlin' - left me crying all night long.

I gave you all my lovin' - gave you my world and everything,
I gave you all my lovin' - gave you my world and everything.
I got nothing to live for baby, left me hanging by a shoestring.

My life is empty without you darlin' I see your face everywhere
My life is empty without you darlin' I see your face everywhere.
I feel so cold and empty honey, I know baby, you don't care!

I sit here, jilted and withdrawn, I got nothing left to lose,
I sit here, jilted and withdrawn, I got nothing left to lose.
But I still got my whisky, smokes and my cheating woman blues.

Marcus Tyler

FOUR TIMES REDUNDANT - PAST IT - JOB SEEKER BLUES

Three times redundant, now four has come along,
Three times redundant, now four has come along
Makes you wonder if it's worth carrying on . . .

Money getting less and less, still got a mortgage to pay
Rates, gas, electricity, still got the mortgage to pay
Look at the bank balance, gets smaller every day . . .

Interviews arranging, there's thirty in the queue
Interviews occurring, still thirty in the queue.
Man behind the big desk wants only one or two . . .

Gender, ethnic, will you fit? That's all they want to know
Can they get you cheaply! They want to know.
Pretty certain in my mind it's age that ends the show . . .

Sitting by the telephone, waiting for the call
At home near the telephone, waiting for the call
Come six o'clock in the evening, the phone's not rang at all . . .

Too young to retire, too old for position, discard
This one's in his fifties, too old for position, discard
Experience, street cred, counts for nought, life's hard . . .

When all seems depression, and you are at your low
Down the bottom, depression, how d'you get so low
Then a call, yes, the job's yours . . . put on your get up and go!

Mike Jackson

STROKE OF MIDNIGHT BLUES

At the stroke of midnight
I saw a phantom dressed in white
And when I saw him
It gave me such a fright.

He walked through the door
He walked through the wall
He walked through the dining room
At the stroke of midnight
I saw a phantom dressed in white

It really kept me thinking
I could not sleep all night
I just kept on praying
For the morning light . . .

Paul Wilkins

SWEET MELODIES

I lie in my bed thinking so deeply of you.
The gentle music brings a tear to my eye
Sweet melodies are forming of you.

I suddenly sit up and burst into tears.
I was thinking of you
I love you so much, too strong to touch
I need you here with me
We would make such a sweet melody

I turn my music up, try and get you out of my head.
It's no good your shadows still there!
My heart and soul need you
Sweet melody, I love you . . .

Kate Susan Douglas

IN THE RUT OF THE WORKING CLASS

Optimism bleeds in the cold light of day
with enduring awe that will not pass away.
Scampering thought vilify the mind,
pounding the pavement like a creature half blind.
A critical tongue beats a raw nerve
as muffled muttering echoes persevere.

Open up fear with a carving knife.
Then acquire a prescription to cope.
Bludgeon the atom of life
or ramble on the surface of hope.
Lungs full of uncertainty
wince under this stratosphere,
while our weather-beaten sanity
lies crawling under the atmosphere.

Oppression kicks in and muffles out.
Jaded screams ruffle and shout.
Starved of oxygen, feeding off emotion
raped of dignity in dilatory motion.
Life drags on and time will pass
in the rut of the working class.

J R Griffiths

FINE LADY
(A tribute to a transsexual)

Elegant lady
How gracefully
You walk down the street
Smart stilettos on your feet
A pretty lace ruff around your neck
Too glamorous
Just for shopping but what the heck
'Are you still coming to the dance?'
You ask
'I'll wear my blue dress I made yesterday
How about you?'
'Don't know yet.' I say
Now the evening has come and your hair looks great
So do your nails beautifully long
And painted red
Mine just break and shred
We pay our money and pass through the door
The band is playing so we take to the floor
You in your blue dress and me in my beige
I'm so proud to be with you
It's as if I'm beside
A star on centre stage
'Good tonight here'
Your comment, your low soft voice
Close to my ear
Well we swing a hip and shake a hand
And I wonder fine lady
If anyone here
Or in all the land
Could ever guess that you
Once were a man . . .

Marda

RAGTIME CITY BLUES

As my old home lets in the rain
And my body is racked in pain
I wish to see the sun, shine.

Streets full of rubbish and brime
Many foul folk who know nothing but crime
I wish to see the sun, shine.

Children scantily dressed and mothers with child
Those innocents left to go completely wild
I wish to see the sun, shine.

Old men bent with trouble and strife
Staring around in fear of their life
I wish to see the sun, shine.

Aged women sidling by
Some with eyes that ask why!
I wish to see the sun, shine.

If only we could wake up one day
With a good Samaritan walking our way
I wish to see the sun, shine.

Glory be to that wonderful soul
Determined to help the pile of human, foul
I wish to see the sun, shine.

One day I hope to move away
And feel the cleanness of a seaside bay
Then, I shall see the sun, shine.

Alma Mongomery Frank

Rosa Canina

If I moved on I feared to lose the love I found with you,
For in the worst years of my life, your love did see me through.

I recovered before you died, when life stood still again,
You couldn't be there as I cried. You couldn't share this pain.

'He was only a dog' someone said. How could they be so cruel.
You'd given me comfort when I felt dead. When survival was a dual.

* * *

 I walked that April by a stream, as one in grief as in a dream.
Earth sang of spring, yet all seemed dark, 'til in the hedge I saw a spark

Of light, of hope - a ray of silver seen in green,
For in the hedgerow I could see, gold pink blushed soft white sheen,

As if especially for me, a wild flower beaming light.
For nestling midst the greenest leaves - a dog rose shone - star bright.

I grasped the stem to pluck the rose. From deep within you screamed
'Please choose, let me go, let me be, love me enough to set me free.'

With stem released I kissed the rose, now peace in my heart I smiled
                                                                                      to know,
All things must change, all seasons move, and somehow this our love
                                                                                      does prove.

* * *

I walk on now for I'm sure your love I'll never lose,
While in the Heavens shines the star - and in the hedge
                      the rose . . .

Anita Richards

HAPPIER TIMES

The world stares
God stares
Why doesn't somebody do something?
My world stops spinning
I have no world
only numbed emotions
I cry
Of course I cry
but no tears fall
My eyes have dried up in the overwhelming heat
There are cameras
and reporters with their food
and rich adornments,
bringing their uninvited western culture,
but no welcome food or water.
They transmit pictures
of this open air museum,
but can they help?
Do they help?
I feel myself emotionally falling
to somewhere better than this.
Somewhere spiritual
Somewhere where I belong;
To happier times . . .

Rob Herd (13)

YOUR LOVE STANDS ETERNALLY

Higher than the highest mountain
Deeper than the deepest sea
Longer than the longest river
Your love flows free to me.

Nothing I can do to earn it
Nothing I can say or do.
Nothing matters more than this
Your love stands eternally.

I will praise your name forever
I was made for your delight
Through the sun and through the showers
Your love stand eternally.

Help me never to forget you
You alone can never fail
Though sometimes you seem far from me
Your love stands eternally.

Nothing can compare to you Lord
Nothing I can ever desire
Though dreams be torn and tattered
Your love stands eternally.

Jacqui Haynes

TOMORROW COMES

Deny the children knowledge
Burn their books and close the schools,
The actions of a government
Of criminals and fools

Suppress the nation's voice
Those questions government finds hard,
But learn to read the signs
Be very much upon your guard

Abuse their human rights
And give them cause for fear and hate,
It is the proof that government
Is merely second-rate

Tomorrow comes and knowledge
Is what youth must always seek
And Burma's young will stop
The havoc current rulers wreak.

Kim Montia

Cumbria

Grey mist surrounds me with its moist gloom,
Enclosing me like a baby in its womb.
Condensation drips from rock slippery wet,
As my lakeland displays another facet
Of its enchanting and variable moods,
While I shelter under a mountain that broods
Protectively over an unrippled lake,
I feel pleasure with every breath I take.

J D Bailey

Gentle Whispers

I heard them singing in the ground.
So pure of note and free,
Then up they rose and turned and smiled,
Sang of the change to be,

The snowdrops and the crocuses,
The daffodils of gold,
Played music and sang softly,
Then tales of wonder told.

They pushed brave heads above the soil,
Commanded by the spring,
Who spread her gown of palest green,
All over everything.

Undaunted she by winter's rage,
She smiled on him instead,
He weakened then and faltered,
Then turned away and fled.

Kathleen M Scatchard

Vapour Trails

Through a generous pane
On a parchment of sky
There's a picture to behold
Mind boggling to the eye
Vapour trails criss cross
Where men appear to fly
Too close to one another
To pass, to and from, by
Parallel, pin point angles
A tapestry in the sky
Unique and artistic
Are these artists who fly . . .

Jack Pritchard

GRAINS OF SAND

Youth and passion go hand in hand,
The years pass by like grains of sand.
Your love is reflected in your face,
In my heart you have a special place.
Little things you say and do,
They all say I love you.
True love will never die,
You'll find it's true as time goes by.
In your middle years, passion fades,
You now recall your golden days.
The sands of time bring sweet repose,
The bud did open into a beautiful rose.

Doreen Fraser

ANTI-SMOKING JINGLES
(Written at the behest of my 9 year old Granddaughter)

Little girls seldom seem to think
And seldom want to learn
Smoking fags will make you stink
Abstaining helps you learn.

Tinker Bell was a fairy
Neither fat nor very hairy
Stinker Bell's skin was variegated
The affliction being smoke-related.

Little Miss Muffet sat on a tuffet
Smoking five fags a day
There came a big spider
Which sat down beside her
Which said *'Phew! Please breathe the other way!'*

Jack and Jill went up the hill for a fag
And a bucket of water
Jack felt sick and came down quick
Whilst Jill washed her mouth out with water.

Smoke is no joke
It stinks on your breath
It stinks on your clothes
It is absolutely filthy
As everybody knows!

She was only the Vicar's daughter
She knew she didn't ought-er
But she smoked ten fags
To be one of the lads
And stank like the Curate's egg after.

She was only the baker's daughter
But she never used her loaf
She smoked by the dozen.
In a baker's oven
And regretted it ever after.

She was only the butcher's daughter
But she never minced her words.
She said 'No' as her mother had taught her.
Annd shouted when she couldn't be heard.

Caroline smoking fags looks fine
All very clandestine
Her morals were never very fine
Her health is now in serious decline.

She said *'Riddle-de-dee and fiddle-de-dee*
Nothing will ever happen to me!'
Her boy friend's gone sailing out to sea
And she is in the mortuary.

Smoking is to be dreaded
Sir Walter Raleigh's beheaded
And justice is done . . .

Robert Catlin

THAT INFAMOUS DAY IN 1941

The rising German Eagle brought terror across Europe.
As countries began their fall the Luftwaffe became a force
                                        to be reckoned with,
Even Italy became Germany's ally before a third party made
                                        it a trio.
Fighting had been raging for over two years when Japan entered
                                        the war.
Japanese diplomats were in Washington assuring peace!
The US Secretary of State in conference with them was a
                                        Mr Cordell Hull.

However war was declared on December 7th 1941.
A quiet Sunday morning erupted into horror, smoke, fire and debris
                                        over Pearl Harbour.
Waves of Japanese aircraft bombed Pearl Island whilst talks were
                                        going on.
It could only be described as a sneak attack as President Roosevelt said
'A date that will live in infamy' it was as vicious as it was sudden.
With serious damage on shore like the sinking of the ship *'Oklahoma'*
including the *'Arizona'* many more were damaged in a raid lasting
                                        110 minutes long.
Within a space of hours the balance of naval power in the Pacific had
                                        been perceptibly altered.
On the first anniversary of the treacherous attack details were unveiled
                                        not known to the public.
Information on the true extent of damage on the battleships, a knockout
                                        blow that wasn't
The number of casualties accounted for heavy losses of more than
                                        three thousand.
Japans declaring of war with America and Britain was true to the
                                        Axis formula.
Of those Japanese lost fifty aircraft were hit showing signs of a
                                        comeback
Showing twenty-eight shot down by the Navy, twenty or more by
                        Army fighters and two machined gunned.

Replacements were due after so many ships and aircraft were out of action.
The American Fleet were to recover with her striking force becoming as strong as ever . . .

Edward G Scullion

A MIND FULL OF YOU . . .

When I woke up this morning,
I thought of you first
When I got up this morning
I need a coffee burst.

When I left the flat this morning,
I saw someone that looked like you,
I did not stop to chat,
Didn't feel the need to.

When I started the car this morning,
The thing did not wanner move,
And guess who I thought of first,
Yes! That's right - you!

When I got to work this morning,
I saw your picture upon my desk,
And that's what made me realise
Just who I love the best . . .

Emma Clark

ON THE EVE...

It was evening, and autumn

We flew the little plane
with its model engine sound
over fields just harvested
the sun behind us.

And there
invisible from the ground
was the outline of a villa.

We sobered, took bearings,
used up all the film
turned back in silent admiration.

The photo came out better
than we'd dared to hope.

And in the corner was the shadow
of the little plane we'd put to better use
than a joy-ride for cadets.

And knowing
we could never follow up
the discovery ourselves
we made up in drink
and called the plan
Minerva's Owl...

John Dixon

TO OUR CHILDREN

My dear and beloved children,
You are now halfway through your path of life.
We know of your sorrows, joy and strife.
Life seems to be one short flight from generation
                                        to generation.
From us to you from you to yours -
You have fought and sought, received and lost,
Hopes were dashed - sometimes at great cost!
Persistence is vital on this walk of life
Disappointments - always there, troubles are rife.
We have travailed and are tired and worn,
Yet still for you all we'll go on and on . . .
Treat life with respect, give your best to all,
But always remember we are here when you call . . .

Georgina Knight

TWO SIDES OF THE COIN
SPOILT

As a child I lived in a small village
There were only three streets
A church a pub and a co-operative store
A school and four farms
On the map it looked a country village
Not too far from the coast.
As you approached the thought was the same
A lovely country place surrounded by green fields
With sun ripened corn and green thorn hedges
Until you noticed between two streets
The iron towers and the turning wheels
The black mountain with an aerial flight
That whirred and clicked and rattled along
Dumping waste from the colliery
That supplied the coal
As the years passed the black heap
Spread until there were no gardens left
The heap creeping up to these houses
The smell on warm days of rotten eggs
Was too unbearable
The dust on dry days almost killed us
Choking our throats and blinding our eyes
Filling our homes with black dirt
Covering the clean washing on the lines
We all remember Aberfan
How many Aberfans might there have been
This colliery village was only one of many
And there by the grace of a God - this village survived!

Joan Smith

AND SO YOU BECOME MY OBSESSION

And so you become my obsession
The subject of my every thought
The reason for my very being.
And I knew it would be like this
Somehow I just knew
From the first time I saw you
And I was struck by your beauty,
The warmth of your eyes
And the gentleness of your voice.

And so you become my obsession
Everything I do is with you in mind
Every word I speak is of you.
And I knew it would be like this
Somehow I just knew,
From the first time we talked
And you caught me in your web of words,
Teased me with your whispers
And the pounding of your heart.

And so you become my obsession
All that I want is to touch you
All that I ask is to hold you.
And I knew it would be like this
Somehow I just knew,
From the first time we kissed
And I was stolen by your lips
Feeling their caress
And the beating of your breath.

And so you become my obsession
Every dream I dream is of you
Every thought I have is yours.
And I knew it would be like this
Somehow I just knew,
From the first time we made love
And I felt your gentle caress
The softness of your skin
And the sweet surrender of your body.

Kelvin Hughes

SHADOW OF DEATH

Down in the depths, the storm is heard
The shadow of death passes by
A huge sea monster created by man
Its belly bulging so full to the brim
The ways is lost for him.

The powers of the sea and mother nature
The massive bulk tosses like a feather
Thrown against the rocks of Earth
Its huge belly erupts, pouring out its jet blood.
Throwing its daggers of wood.

Surfacing from the depths below, the creatures rise
Being tossed like rag dolls
The manic storm, the raging bull
The floundering bulk out of control
Guts spilled everywhere, like man on patrol.

The tiny birds struggle with last breath
Feather ruined no return to take
Infants not having a chance of life
Thrown at mans mistake
Hours before he's to wake.

Destructive storm to a mocking calm breeze
Leaving behind the mess
The sea of death, like the remnants of black plague
Another major warning to man
The death of his planets began.

Carole Saberton

WANDERING THOUGHTS

I had a startling thought just now -
Something to write a poem about
But it went as suddenly as it came
I cannot recall it - my mind is lame.
It stumbles and halting wonders how
And whence came the thought my wandering found.

Do words and thoughts drift and hover around
Seeking a haven, a mind to use?
Do words from the past forever intrude
Can we take credit when ideas abound
Have our *inspirations* existed before?

The exciting idea I had just now
Was gone before I could hold it.
If only I'd made a note of it
I could reach out my mind and enfold it,
And out of the union of mystic and mind
Might have issued a masterpiece
No one knows how!

A I Darwin

LOST LOVE

This is the pivot of the orbit of my life
And now it is gone.
And like a bombarded neutron,
I fly into the outer space of life
Into that cold place where there is no love nor affection.
Hell must be a cold place!

Into that crazy vastness where no pattern is discernible,
Where harmony disintegrates
Into shards of cold idiocy.
Where wretched, jogging, mumbo-jumbo
Panics and shreds the mind.
Hell is a cold place!

Pain is pain and cold and heat fall into one.
Seared, the mind whirls
And flaps in gibbering nothingness.
Sanity must blindfold and stagger for it's balance
On that spinning ice,
In that cold hell!

J J S Clare

THE TEARS I CRY...

Beneath the surface of my smile,
there lurks a silent tear
But no-one in this world would guess
And no-one wants to hear.
How many raw emotions hide
Beneath the surface of a smile?

Behind the veil of laughter,
There lies an aching heart
But others just don't want to know.
That is the hardest part.
Can a broken heart survive hereafter
Behind a veil of laughter?

So ask me how I'm feeling
And I'll answer with a lie
For no-one really wants to know
About the tears I cry.

Rosemary Thomson

IN MY DREAMS...

In my dreams you come to me
With sweet times of used to be.
Once again your arms enfold
To shield me from the bitter cold
Of the world that now I see.

As you kiss me tenderly
Love and laughter set me free
And my body is not old
In my dreams.

We run across the sunlit lea
And walk beside the timeless sea.
Joined as one by a band of gold,
You still are mine to have and hold.
As we were, we shall always be
In my dreams . . .

Margaret Banfield

Storm Dog

Growling of the thunder hound,
All other noise beneath it drowned,
A deep and doleful warning sound,
Beware the lightning bite.

Frantic trees relay the warning,
Batten down and wait for morning,
Bringing peace, a calmer dawning,
Tames the Storm Dogs' might.

Howling winds, the following pack,
Calling out behind his back,
As each one senses Storm Dogs' track,
And howls to join the fight.

Lashing rain, their marker scent,
Telling all which way they went,
Then finally the storm is spend,
Until another night.

Gill Shutt

THE LOVER

Mr and Mrs Smith, we signed
Of course, that was only pretend.
For we weren't married, though I knew you well,
It was only a means to an end.
I little guessed when I made the suggestion,
That with my plan, you would agree.
It really was only make a joke
Never thought that you'd say *'Yes.'* to me.
You told me that you would try anything once,
When you said that - I thought that you bluffed
But you said *'Yes I'm game, I don't mind if I do!'*
Believe me - I really felt chuffed . . .

I know that it's just a sign of the times
What young people, unwed, do today.
But this was something quite new to us,
Clandestine, exciting, risqué.
At the hotel, I booked the honeymoon suite,
For a day and a night of sheer bliss.
I can still feel the beat of your heart close to mine,
And the warmth of your passionate kiss.
My wildest fantasies, all coming true,
On the beach, as we strolled, hand in hand.
The world was my oyster and you were my pearl
As you laid in my arms, in the sand . . .

Later on in the restaurant, I couldn't eat
The set four course meal was no fun.
I only had appetite just for one thing
And it wasn't for steak, cooked - half done.

Remember that pretty, pink nightie you took
Put it on and then said *'What the heck!*
I might as well not put the thing on at all,
It'll only end up round my neck!'
The memory of that weekend, my love
Will for all of eternity, thrill me,
I only hope I don't talk in my sleep,
If the wife ever finds out - she'll kill me . . .

David Kellard

A Womb With A View...

I've had a spot of bother
Not been too well of late!
Nothing very serious
A feminine complaint.
A hysterectomy was called for
But the outcome isn't bleak.
The surgeon called it routine,
I'll be going home next week!
He told me all about it,
Said not to worry; I'll be fine!
But it's not *his nether regions!*
Being rearranged - *but mine!*
He couldn't possibly appreciate
The feelings of despair.
At the thought of having bits removed,
Especially down there!
It may be just routine to him,
He does it all the time,
But it makes me feel so incomplete
Redundant - passed my prime!
The organ that has been removed,
I feel I have to mourn,
It held my babies safe,
Until the day that they were born!
It was my very essence,
And must not be denied,
I grieve because a part of me
Has had its life, and died!
But I mustn't get too maudlin'
Life goes on, or so they say
And with the help of hormone patches,
Things look brighter every day!

I look forward to some *TLC*
To lift me from my gloom,
In the bosom of my family,
That were once held in my womb . . . !

D Winder

THE LAST GOODBYE

Before I say goodbye
I want to see you
Before I say goodbye
I want to hold you
Before I say goodbye
I want to tell you my fear
Before I say goodbye
I want to know you'll be there
In that beautiful place, called heaven - above
Where peace and tranquillity
Spells happiness and love
Where the trials of the world
Are finally laid to rest
Before I say goodbye
I want you to know
I'll always be there for you . . .

Margaret Luckett-Curtis

THE MIRROR

Reflections of what you look like
Images you really don't want to see.
I stare at my mirror
And I wish I didn't see me.

Wondering how to escape,
Knowing you look the same each day.
Hoping of not waking up
Praying to change some day

Kaja Jarosz

FEELING INFERIOR - FEELING SUPERIOR

Before the judge, the poetic sun
Great writers stand full tall
Yet I do melt, into shade I crawl
Away from the judging line I run.

Priceless poet who I can not but admire
Nor hide from you my genuine awe,
Guide me, teach me the famous tours,
From which reels of verses they can inspire.

Lead me to a sentimental scene,
Though my body may not feel its air.
An innocent, thoughtful mind I will wear
'Til images make my eyes full gleam.

That gleam will be the reflection
Of the sweet sonnet-filled sun
And amongst my great peer, as one,
I will stand and be judged with poetical perfection.

C Sharrock

A SLIGHTLY BROKEN MAN...

The spastic man in front of me
Was only slightly so:
A slightly inturned foot, a hand
Whose slightly claw-like fingers clutched a bag.
His walk was odd, no more than that,
But, added to his long lank hair
And scruffy jeans,
I felt from where I was
Behind him, never having seen his face,
A slight revulsion, shaped by fear,
And as I overtook, in spite of me,
I gave him just a slightly widened berth . . .

Alan Parr

IN THE KEY OF LOVE

God said p*lease* so the angels sang
The treble clef sprung to life,
Breeze played flute, warmth stroked the strings
And drum was banged by ice.

God laughed with joy and kindly asked
For a drop of celestial peace.
As angels soothed the sleeping world
God heard an anxious p*lease!*

God wondered who and found out where
And lifted to his knee
An angel, sad in heaven's house
For he sang out of key.

'My son, you are most welcome here!
My lamb, why do you weep?'
God heard not a more odd reply:
'I do not earn my keep!'

'My messenger, my earthly hand,
My song, my God-like man,
If you do love with angel heart
Live here you must and can!'

The angel gazed down to his cloud
And bravely raised his head.
'I cannot stay, for when I sing
I'm not in tune!' he said.

God pondered this, and asked the rest
'How do you sing so well?'
He tried his own voice, sent it back
And prayed the angels tell.

'We sing because when you say *please*
Our love conquers our lungs
The words and notes abundant flow
And praise rolls off our tongues.'

Then God knelt down with eyes so stern,
Looked in the angel's soul.
'Child, if you love - stay near and sing
As my good choir has told.'

Silent sat the angel-child
While he searched through his heart.
When he rose his eyes were true:
'I love, I'll sing my part.'

Then smiling God said *please* again
Music caressed his ears
As sang each angel from his heart
Through joyful, loving tears.

Anna Louise Simpson

PICTURE NEGATIVES

Waking with dreams
Trickling to the forefront of memory,
Trying to grasp the after-shadows,
Wondering if I remembered in words
Or in Technicolor pictures.
When as a child I wondered
Where sat the source of dreams
I thought of a film reel;
The cut and taped trappings of the day
Projected onto the canvas of my eyelids
Erased each morning by exposure
To the bright light occupying my wake,
But now I know that dreams
Are cultivated somewhere in the conscience
With the projectionist hand-picking
Scenes I would have torn
From the pages of any script . . .

John Bicker

WAR AND TROUBLE

For those troubled spots around the world
we need to find the cause.
To try and bring an end to this
with a decent set of laws.

We find that politics and religion
are the sources that's to blame.
As there are many disagreements here
which brings about this shame.

Deaths that are the result of this
should be by everyone rejected.
For even though of different faiths
friendships are what's expected.

We are creatures of the human race
with brains above all others.
Why do we take the assassins route
to kill those who are our brothers.

Lachlan Taylor

STUKAS AT 8 O'CLOCK AND 4 O'CLOCK

Stukas got the bus, usually first
all that would dare precede them
a brutal reputation, worse
not that they leaned on one
surely *no fear* their creation and curse

Stukas treating people bad, real bad
catholic and poor it appeared
(presumed more than actual fact)
pursued their psycho-flight-path through
real-world unflinching drama no abstract

Stukas on a bombing run hurt you good
crazy they preyed like foxes
we were chickens cooped
seated stiff immobile satchels grasped
fearing treatment to be meted en-route

Stukas characteristics alien to me
strange then how the youngest
opened to the same heart-key
the dark girl of fantasy rebuffing me
quickly, kindly (in the class of '73?)

Stukas - never saw them in action
mind didn't want to much
enacted cautions a fraction
too pointed to ignore like
doubt-burned blazer on a journey's pained protraction

Stukas demanded respect and you could tell
cogent thought embedded too
pile-driven deep in the well
shared fantasy become woman with child
grown up teenager, will the spirit be quelled?

Stukas kind of gone now, school too
no more homicidal head-butts
courtesy of that dive-bombing crew
but such vivid memories
of institutions fashioned as a zoo

Stukas then, brothers two to my three
lasting impression surpassing dire-feared unknowns
maybe a malevolent psyche gratuity
warped and wefted
foster-home-fistedly-crafted
epitomised sixties baby boom blessed
by governments successively (successfully).
Stukas lives totally shafted

- it's sad to admit but
their psycho-MO
was perfectly adapted . . .

Ian R Margetts

ON THE SWEET COUCH OF YOUTH

On the sweet couch of youth,
With soft beguiling
Time seduces us
Whispers earnestly all
Promises to fulfil all
Ambitions to be met
Sprinkles Ecstasy over all
Our dreams.
Crowns our head with
Fancies, and
Feeds the hunger of our
Needs, but . . .
Lonelier and dreadfuller than
Death
Withdrawal finds us deep
In the nightmare of
Old age.
Our magic and our beauty and our strength
All gone.
Time mocks our foolishness and
Hurries to our door the
Ungrieving hearse to take us
To finality.
Why can't life be fitted with
Reverse?
Run back like children
To the start,
Promise to be better,
Hand on heart,

Again and again to
Run the race, to hone
Our spirit, and
At last to trace
The sweet return to
It's special place.

John Parry

Fall

These broken sentences make no pretence at rhythm or rhyme
or structure
These are merely the outlet the countless hooks tugging at my
fractured soul
Saying them doesn't banish them or bring you back to me
In face I can't see the point
But I can't see the point in anything anymore, so I continue on regardless
I wish this expression was unnecessary, but this is not just another
sad story
It is my destruction
Euthanasia would be my only release from the rusty spikes piercing
my heart
But you have trapped me with the pain
Because I cannot inflict the guilt and hurt I know you would feel
If I took the easy route out to annihilation
So you force me down on this bed of nails
Hurt blasting through boundaries past the stage of tears and insanity
Beyond the anger you all beg me to feel
For if I hate you because I love you
The self-revulsion may be too much for me to stand
So I embrace despair and frozen memories
Let the agonising wound slowly heal over
A gaping hole beneath
But of course you return to me as a half-life friend
Just enough to aggravate the bleeding again
Your smile, your laugh, your eyes
Something I need so dearly
But cannot fully resurrect
It's only been a few days, but already a decade
Like the unimaginable gulf between us

And I so wish I had seen the cracks of this rift before it opened
Done what I could, tried to stop common ground crumbling
You tell me it's not my fault
That your feelings changed
But it is so confusing to me
So strange to me when we shared such passion in the onset
That at the end I am alone with my grief
You don't feel it too!
But tell me you have felt it before
Then why am I not good enough for you to feel it for me?
Why couldn't you fight to save us?
I would have never dreamed of giving up, struggled through the night
All my efforts meant nothing, everything I have given you have
                                                            taken away
Melancholy thoughts, chances never to be
Pain over the wrong opportunities, stepping possibly too far when
I thought it would last forever.
Fear that I might betray the remembrance of this unrequited emotion
With someone less deserving
I am so desperate to escape this pit
When each second brings a thought of you
And each second bangs in a tormenting stasis
But when I struggled onto the marble step back to a life however empty
I looked back from this elevated vantage point
And saw what I had lost
The step dissolving beneath me
And once more I fall to oblivion
Reaching out despairingly to catch the one thing that remains
A misplaced faith in you, to be held through the plummet to
                                                            dark eternity.

James Conder

GITA...

She brought a little light
To the way I was.

She opened the door
To the darkness.

I could see her
As she walked through the night.

I could touch her
As if she was there.

My fair maiden
With her long golden hair.

If only she was alive
To pave the cities in gold.

She would do the rest
And they would do as they were told.

She brought me much pleasure
When I was with her,
Washing my sins away
While night turned to day.

She saw the enemy in my eyes
Like the first time
I had told her
One of my many lies.

Never love, but passion
Resting inside
To perfect the intensity
As she lay down and cried.

Now I see her for real
Caged in a landscape
Where lovers drift
And mountains collide.

Now I wait for the moment
When I watch her fly
Like a dove
Across a deep blue sky.

I awake at dawn
To a chorus of angels
Singing to cure
Man of his vehement scorn.

Now I need her
To nurture my peace
So that my love for Gita
Will one day increase.

I cultivate a place
For her to put her head
Living in the depths of man
Living with the dead.

Despite her fear
I will always be free
To love her nature
To wait for the time
When God is mine
And my mind is clear.

Graham Hardie

LOVE MATCH

Then there was love
there was deep power
in the body controlled
by an agile mind
the lady of his love
joked and said it
was just one sided
there was nothing that
could be done to
enhance the love match
the love match was
her and those very
ladylike ways she had
found over the years
her way was hid
till he saw all
her many hidden secrets
she was reborn again
that love magic was
a strong old desire
he had it as well
in some smaller ways
his never ever showed
true dark promise is
mostly often hid so
they will often say
trouble is we love
its a hard life
even so harder with
one you just love.

Richard Clewlow

THE THINGS I WISH I KNEW

These are the things I wish I knew:
the thoughts of the sun,
of birds and hills and fields,
the thoughts of the trees
and the sky, the prayers
of the long silver nights,
the carols of each season,
for then my heart would be
a poet very close to God.

Marion Schoeberlein

MORE TIME

Her life's half done
and time is running out,
seems to accelerate.
Played out her part
in the multiplying saga
of dear life,
in duplicate.
But she was meant for more
and before now
She should have done:
Shared all the music
in her soul
till it was gone;
Captured,
until the last good word
floating in mind,
on plate -
Her life,
the world,
and points of view.
Of things she knows
in full, in part,
and those we speculate about.
Oh no!
She cannot die
until her work is done.
More time besides
to savour and appreciate.
But here she lies,
where she fell
between two stools.
She must create
before the curtain falls.

Carolyn Long

WE LIVE IN DIFFICULT TIMES . . .

Never before has the human had to live like we do live now
                                                                     at the present time!
We lost the meaning of the word friendship and to forgive and
                                                                      forget!
I did a few times and for this I am very happy.
Especially this time of Christmas and the New Year.
If you can forgive and forget you will gain the friendship and
                                                                      the respect.
And also you have done the good deed for the past and the
                                                                     future years.
We never know in our life when we do need a friendship!
If there is no friend to lend you a hand.
No one will pick you up if you fall down in the gutter!
My experience of life is that a good friend is worth more
                                                                 than thousands of pounds.
Many times money can do nothing for you but a good and sincere
                                                       friend is better than anything!
And forgive and forget for all of us is the best we must do in this world,
Forgive and forget - if we wish to have God's help.
And the respect of our brothers and sisters
Whom we live together with on this Earth . . .

Antonio Martorelli

Confusion

In our confusion,
we suffer delusion,
or, make an illusion,
suffice for solution.

But, what of creation
is there such a nation,
with thought penetration,
to halt deviation?

What sort of suggestion,
comes begging the question,
has all common action,
no dis-satisfaction!

Is there some compunction,
that makes us disfunction,
or, has our life function,
arrived at some junction?

Will we go on in complete elation,
or, fall apart in utter frustration,
mixing up good and bad was temptation,
only the truth can be our salvation.

What is the truth? It's all radiation,
causing our brain all this aberration,
it will take lots of determination,
to save us all from contamination.

Jean Paisley

ABERFAN

When I gaze o'er the valley from my home,
I can see the mountain clearly.
And I know that where e're I may roam,
My homeland I will ever think of dearly.

On its green slopes sheep graze peacefully,
Only the trees cast shadows in the sun,
It seems not long since we sat tearfully,
When a coal-tip moved and took both old and young.

A strange silence on the mountain then took place.
Where sound of chain on tram was often heard before,
On the peak appeared an outline of a face
Of the man who shared the sorrow that we bore.

It is not easy to comprehend
When disaster strikes fast.
It's a comfort to have a good friend,
Whose friendship we know will last.

'Tis to Jesus our Saviour we turn,
For we know he will understand,
It is then only then, we will learn,
When we all take him by the hand.

Cyril George Button

TO A VERY SPECIAL MUM AND DAD

Our family plays a big part
in how we live today.
Our Mum and Dad especially
they set us on our way.

They always showed us loving
in a happy family home.
Their selflessness and caring
could never be outdone.

As a family unit,
when we were all so young.
We were taught to love each other
no matter what we'd done.

OK we had our fighting
as families always do.
But when I look back to those times,
our love was always true.

And now that we are older
with families of our own.
We still love each other dearly
it will never be outgrown.

But there is something special
in all the things we do.
We owe that to our Mum and Dad
we all love you, through and through.

Your loving and your kindness
it is still playing a big part.
We are never treated differently,
you have it down to a fine art.

We very much appreciate
all the things that you do.
However would we manage
without our Mum and Dad
Thank you . . . !

Julie Wilkins

CATS AND DOGS

A small girl - not so free
But she's lonely; unlike me!
Her frail dog shivers and begs,
Newspaper covers their thin blue legs.

I think my England can't be alone.
Children everywhere looking for a bone.
This world they say, is a perfect place,
On the face of sadness - can this be the case!

Cats like tigers, do roam free.
They're a bit like you, a bit like me.
Street-life for them is not unkind
Snug and warm - I think you'll find!

I look at this sight in constant amuse
And think of some parents, whom forever abuse.
Why must she beg, at this innocent age
Better in my eyes, to turn another page.

My mother and friend, stop talking at last.
As we slither away, through crowds that are vast.
Thinking of home, what a day that had been.
Poor girl, and poor dog, and setting my own clothes
Out - clean . . .

Michelle Widdrington (9)

CHILDREN!

Carl stop pulling Sophie's hair
Luke get away from those stairs.
I've told you all be quiet and sit
Oh Lord! Why do I baby-sit?

Jack don't crayon on that wall.
Marc get down before you fall.
Jimmy it's not nice to spit,
Oh Lord! Why do I baby-sit?

Now children wash and go to bed
You would not listen to what I've said.
You wouldn't stop, you wouldn't quit
Oh Lord! Why do I baby-sit?

As I look down at sleeping faces
They make me think of heavenly places.
So adorably cute, they've got me smitten
The pleasure I get from baby-sitting . . .

David Strauss Steer

INSIDERS

How bright that morning were your eyes:
Open windows, hiding nothing,
Bold, bewitching and beguiling.

I pledged my place within their spell:
No words were said, none were needed,
No conditions sought or ceded.

Both slave and master would I be:
But other eyes were there to see
Invading our intimacy.

Sharp eyes shafting sideways glances
Saying stranger why are you here!
Go away - do not interfere!

Green eyes flashing hate and envy:
Revealing needs long unresolved,
Longing to love and to be loved.

Contemptuous eyes coldly staring:
Sneering at signs of devotion,
Scorning such shows of emotion.

Thus it was the spell was broken:
Our dream now a fatality
Never to know reality . . .

Kenneth Wilcox

RHAPSODY OF THE RAT RACE

Chittering, chattering, wheeling and dealing.
The sounds of the city annoyingly press on.
With a glance at their Rolex watches,
Consulting their travel timetables:
Time for nothing to do with you or me,
Railing in lines to collect wage cheques,
Reeking their ballads from sad cafes,
All hunger and thirst will be resolved
By an all day breakfast,
Sincerely yours for £1.99
Where are our hearts now
My pretty child?
Shall we close them in a divine effort?
To enhance at a glance our consumer values.

Four in the afternoon
No altercation
All stretches of imagination confined
In the tin cages of taxis, waiting in anticipation.
Shall I prepare all of my life?
In such meticulous detail forsake my imagination
To reach out and touch conformity.
In the Take Aways the chips depravingly fry in their fat,
My words trickle down in their soporific sound
From their womb of a wound I have no intention to heal
Nightfall
The clockwork city sleeps forever in her indifference.
The lights are grey and dim in the tower blocks
Oh Lord! Let us delve deeply.
Please Lord let us pretend
Dear Lord bring us to forgive . . .

Sean Conway

TO A YOUNG GERMAN SAILOR

We had been waiting for you for a long time,
After the klaxon sounded the red alert in the night
And the depth charges echoed their outrage
Against the petrol-loaded tanks beneath our feet.

Then in the early morning, the sun sparkling and the sea
Blue and windblown white, we who were weary from lack of sleep.
But alive could see the escorts flurrying ahead of the convoy
And raised a cheer as a destroyer sped from astern down the line.

Excitement leavened my sixteen-year-old terror
As the depth charges thundered the morning away.
The flags fluttering aloft the masts and the Aldis lamps
Flashing the news of a sinking ahead.

From focsle and mess deck we came to line the rails.
Watching for the tell-tale signs of oil or debris but aware
The old submariner's trick of gifting these to fool
The escorts so they'd go away.

They came, the debris, shining oil, odd garments, then
The galley muck, but nothing which convinced.
Until behind, lifting with wind and spume, swept on each bow wave,
Ship to ship the unmistakable reality that authorised success.

White roll-necked sweater, dead young face, and you, the enemy
Bobbed idly by while we, momentary victors, watched
All silent now until you disappeared astern,
Alone, they say, until the sea gives up its dead . . .

John Finch

MOTHER'S ROOM...

Underneath the clutter upstairs in mother's room
I'm sure there must be treasure or an old heirloom.
There's piles of clothes
There's stax of books
There's old photographs
There's probably spooks!
It'll take forever to clear a space
'Cos she can clutter for the human race.
From every charity shop in town
She'll purchase things without a frown.
She fills the house with odds and sods.
Like a tribal offering to the Gods.
We have to clear a path to bed
So that I can rest my weary head.
Then I can dream that when I wake
I've not been caught in an earthquake
But in the morning when I rise
I focus on that elusive prize.
Pile for pile, measure for measure
Somewhere near . . . there must be treasure!

Derek (Dovann) Blackburn

THIS EASTER

This Easter
may the stone roll away
from the dark of your cave.

This Easter
may the depths of your soul
see a light within.

This Easter
may these words of wisdom
light your journey through life.

(And for God's sake - cheer up!)

Kendric Ross

SUBMISSIONS INVITED
SOMETHING FOR EVERYONE

POETRY NOW '99 - Any subject, any style, any time.

WOMENSWORDS '99 - Strictly women, have your say the female way!

STRONGWORDS '99 - Warning! Age restriction, must be between 16-24, opinionated and have strong views. (Not for the faint-hearted)

All poems no longer than 30 lines. Always welcome! No fee! Cash Prizes to be won!

Mark your envelope (eg *Poetry Now)* **'99**
Send to:
Forward Press Ltd
Remus House, Coltsfoot Drive,
Woodston, Peterborough, PE2 9JX

OVER £10,000 POETRY PRIZES TO BE WON!

Judging will take place in October 1999